W9-AFR-226

Washington, D.C.

Jim Ollhoff

Visit us at
www.abdopublishing.com

Published by ABDO Publishing Company, 8000 West 78th Street, Suite 310, Edina, Minnesota 55439 USA. Copyright ©2010 by Abdo Consulting Group, Inc. International copyrights reserved in all countries. No part of this book may be reproduced in any form without written permission from the publisher. The Checkerboard Library™ is a trademark and logo of ABDO Publishing Company.

Printed in the United States.

Editor: John Hamilton
Graphic Design: Sue Hamilton
Cover Illustration: Neil Klinepier
Cover Photo: iStock Photo

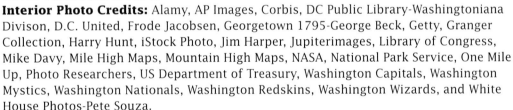

Manufactured with paper containing at least 10% post-consumer waste

Interior Photo Credits: Alamy, AP Images, Corbis, DC Public Library-Washingtoniana Divison, D.C. United, Frode Jacobsen, Georgetown 1795-George Beck, Getty, Granger Collection, Harry Hunt, iStock Photo, Jim Harper, Jupiterimages, Library of Congress, Mike Davy, Mile High Maps, Mountain High Maps, NASA, National Park Service, One Mile Up, Photo Researchers, US Department of Treasury, Washington Capitals, Washington Mystics, Washington Nationals, Washington Redskins, Washington Wizards, and White House Photos-Pete Souza.
Statistics: State population statistics taken from 2008 U.S. Census Bureau estimates. City and town population statistics taken from July 1, 2007, U.S. Census Bureau estimates. Land and water area statistics taken from 2000 Census, U.S. Census Bureau.

Library of Congress Cataloging-in-Publication Data

Ollhoff, Jim, 1959-
  Washington, D.C. / Jim Ollhoff.
     p. cm. -- (The United States)
  Includes bibliographical references and index.
  ISBN 978-1-60453-684-3 (alk. paper)
  1. Washington (D.C.)--Juvenile literature. I. Title.

  F194.3.O44 2009
  975.3--dc22
                        2008052875

THOMAS CRANE PUBLIC LIBRARY
QUINCY MA

CITY APPROPRIATION

Table of Contents

The District...4

Quick Facts 6

Geography 8

Climate and Weather 12

The Cherry Trees 14

History..18

People 24

The National Mall 28

The White House 34

Transportation..36

Industry 38

Sports 40

Entertainment..42

Timeline...44

Glossary...46

Index..48

The District

   Washington, D.C., is not a state. It is a piece of land called a federal district. It is the home of the United States government. The government moved to Washington, D.C., in 1800. Thousands of people have government jobs, and most work in Washington, D.C. It is a beautiful city, filled with monuments, museums, and historic places to visit.

   Washington, D.C., is sometimes nicknamed "D.C.," or "the District." Washington is named after the first president of the United States. D.C. stands for District of Columbia. When the government decided it needed a place for a capital, it was called the District of Columbia. It was meant to honor Christopher Columbus, the European explorer who sailed to America in 1492.

Fireworks light up the sky during a Washington, D.C., celebration.

Quick Facts

Name: Washington is named after President George Washington. District of Columbia is named after Christopher Columbus.

Date of Creation: Founded in 1790. The United States government officially moved there in 1800.

Population: 591,833

Area (Total Land and Water): 68.3 square miles (177 sq km)

Nicknames: D.C., or the District

Motto: *Justitia omnibus* (Justice to all)

Official Bird: Wood Thrush

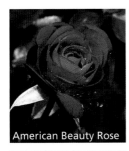
American Beauty Rose

Scarlet Oak

Potomac River

Official Flower: American Beauty Rose

Official Tree: Scarlet Oak

Official Song: "The Star-Spangled Banner"

Highest Point: Point Reno, 409 ft (125 m)

Lowest Point: Potomac River, 0 ft (0 km)

Average July Temperature: 79°F (26°C)

Record High Temperature: 106°F (41°C), July 20, 1930

Average January Temperature: 35°F (2°C)

Record Low Temperature: -15°F (-26°C), February 11, 1899

Average Annual Precipitation: 39 in (99 cm)

Number of U.S. Senators: None

Number of U.S. Representatives: None

U.S. Postal Service Abbreviation: DC

Geography

Maryland borders Washington, D.C., on the northwest, northeast, and southeast sides of the city. The Potomac River runs along the southwest side of the city. Across the river is the state of Virginia.

The Anacostia River cuts through the District of Columbia,

The Anacostia River cuts through the city of Washington, D.C.

running northeast to southwest. Three reservoirs supply water for the city. They are the Dalecarlia Reservoir, the McMillan Reservoir, and the Georgetown Reservoir. Many parts of the city used to be swampland.

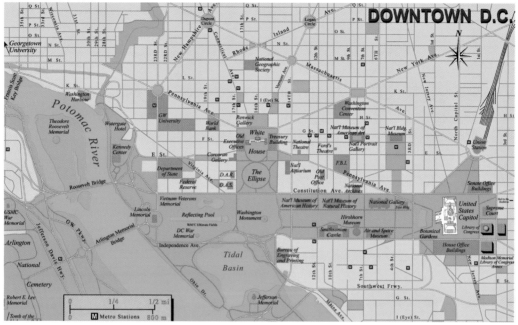

Washington, D.C.'s total land and water area is 68.3 square miles (177 sq km). It is the capital of the United States.

The highest point in Washington, D.C., is Point Reno, in the neighborhood of Tenleytown, in the northwest part of the city. It is 409 feet (125 m) above sea level. The lowest point is at sea level, along the Potomac River.

When the city of Washington was first created in the 1790s, it was one of several cities in the District of Columbia. The District also included the villages of Georgetown, Alexandria, and Hamburgh. The new capital was created between these villages. It was originally called the Federal City. Its name was changed in 1791 to honor the nation's first president, George Washington.

In 1791, President Washington hired French architect Pierre L'Enfant to design the city. L'Enfant placed the Capitol building in the center. He then connected the buildings of the government with long, straight avenues. This was a symbol that the parts of the United States government were separate, but still connected.

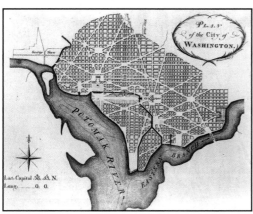

Above, a May 2006 orbital view of Washington, D.C., taken by a NASA crewmember aboard the International Space Station. Clearly visible are the long, straight avenues planned by city architect Pierre L'Enfant in 1791. His original drawing (left) shows the Capitol building in the center of the city.

Climate and Weather

Washington, D.C., has cool winters. An average winter sees about 16 inches (41 cm) of snow. In winter, low temperatures average about 25 degrees Fahrenheit (-4°C).

Summers are humid and hot. High temperatures average about 90 degrees Fahrenheit (32°C). The area's heat and humidity often lead to thunderstorms. These storms can be so strong that they sometimes create tornados.

Spring and fall are pleasant and mild in Washington, D.C. There is lower humidity during these seasons.

While rare, hurricanes sometimes make their way toward Washington, D.C. Because the city is inland, and it is north of where most hurricanes hit, hurricanes do little damage except for heavy rains.

Summers can be hot and humid, often leading to thunderstorms in the nation's capital.

Winters are cool in Washington, D.C. Occasionally, a heavy snowfall strikes the city.

The Cherry Trees

A very popular Washington, D.C., tourist attraction is the city's huge collection of cherry trees. The National Cherry Blossom Festival is held each year in the spring, when the trees are in full bloom.

The story of the Washington, D.C., cherry trees began in 1885. A writer named Eliza Ruhamah Scidmore returned from a trip to Japan. In Japan, the cherry tree is an important flowering plant.

Eliza Scidmore

Back home, Scidmore talked to government officials about planting cherry trees in Washington, D.C. She kept talking about her idea, and many years later, it finally happened.

In 1909, the people of Japan gave 2,000 cherry trees to the United States to be planted

In 1909, as a symbol of friendship, Japan gave 2,000 cherry trees to the United States to be planted in the nation's capital.

in Washington, D.C. Japan wanted to symbolize the friendship between Japan and the United States.

Unfortunately, in 1910, biologists discovered that the cherry trees were infested with harmful insect pests and plant diseases. The biologists were afraid the pests and the diseases would spread to other trees in the United States. All the trees were burned to destroy the infestation.

American officials were afraid that the Japanese would be insulted by the burning of the trees. But Japanese officials were not insulted. In fact, they gave even more trees. This time, the Japanese government gave more than 3,000 trees to the United States.

President and Mrs. Taft.

In 1912, the wives of President William Howard Taft and the Japanese ambassador planted the first two cherry trees in Washington, D.C. The two original trees are still standing today. The trees are especially beautiful in West Potomac Park, where they frame such monuments as the Jefferson Memorial, the Korean War Veterans Memorial, and the Franklin Delano Roosevelt Memorial.

Beginning in 1927, schoolchildren began reenacting the 1912 tree planting. Within a few years, the National Cherry Blossom Festival had grown into an annual three-day celebration. By the 1990s, the festival had grown to be two weeks long. Hundreds of thousands of people come to see the beautiful trees each spring.

Beautiful cherry blossoms surround the Jefferson Memorial.

History

Before European settlers arrived, Native Americans had lived in the Washington, D.C., area for hundreds of years. The Piscataway Indians lived on the north side of the Potomac River, and the Powhatan Indians lived on the south side. As European settlers arrived, the Native Americans were pushed farther to the west.

In the early 1700s, a handful of villages sprang up along the Potomac River in the area that is today Washington,

D.C. Georgetown became an official town in 1751. It was on the Maryland side of the river. The village of Hamburgh was settled near the riverfront swamps known today as Foggy Bottom. Alexandria, Virginia, south of the Potomac River, was established in 1749.

In 1783, the United States won its independence from England. Lawmakers in Congress decided that a permanent capital for the new nation was needed. Congress argued about where the national capital should be. All the states wanted the capital on their soil.

In 1790, Congress decided that the capital should be on federal land, not part of a state. The lawmakers created a 10-mile (16-km) square site along the Potomac River. President George Washington picked the exact spot of the new capital. Both Maryland and Virginia gave up land for the site.

Washington and architect Pierre L'Enfant picked out the spot of the nation's capital.

The federal government moved to Washington in 1800. The city had hard times at first. In 1814, during the War of 1812, the British burned many of the city's buildings, including the White House and the Capitol. During the Civil War (1861–1865), the city of Washington was threatened several times by Confederate forces.

On August 24, 1814, British forces set fire to the White House and the Capitol. People fled the city.

In 1847, the land south of the Potomac River was returned to Virginia. And, in 1871, the city of Washington took over Georgetown and other cities still within the District of Columbia. The city of Washington and the District of Columbia were now one and the same. The city's name became Washington, D.C.

In the late 1800s and early 1900s, many of the city's famous buildings were built. These included the Library of Congress, the Lincoln Memorial, and the Washington Monument.

By 1900, the population of Washington, D.C., was more than 250,000. The city grew much larger than originally planned. People began to drive automobiles, which made the city grow in size even more. World War I and World War II forced the government to spend more money. The government needed to hire many new workers. This also caused the city to grow.

Construction of the Library of Congress Thomas Jefferson Building was completed in 1897. Today, the building is one of three Library of Congress sites.

In 1990, a homeless man slept on a steam grate by the White House.

The growth of Washington, D.C., eventually became a big problem. By the 1990s, city services had grown old, and the federal government hadn't provided enough money. The city's finances had been mismanaged or wasted. In 1995, Congress created a special board to oversee the finances of the city. This supervision was stopped in 2001 after the city balanced its budgets. Today, Washington, D.C., continues to struggle against crime and poverty, just like most big cities. But many parts of the city have greatly improved. Today, more and more people enjoy the city's culture, history, and quality of life.

Washington, D.C., is a highly visible center of power in the world. That sometimes makes it a target for people who commit violence. On September 11, 2001, terrorists hijacked a plane and crashed it into the Pentagon, the headquarters of the U.S. Department of Defense. The Pentagon is on federal land in Arlington County, Virginia, just across the Potomac River. The attack killed 125 people in the Pentagon, and all 64 people on the airplane. This was part of a terrorist attack that also struck the World Trade Center in New York City.

The Pentagon underwent repairs in 2001-2002 after terrorists hijacked a plane and crashed it into the building.

People

Duke Ellington (1899–1974) was one of the most famous musicians of the 1900s. Born in Washington, D.C., he started taking piano lessons at age seven. He became an expert in several musical styles. He and his band played jazz, big band, ragtime, swing, and other styles. He wrote a lot of music, and he often combined musical styles. His band toured the United States and other countries from the 1920s until his death in 1974. He is often simply called "The Duke."

Samuel L. Jackson (1948–) is an American actor. He was active in the civil rights movement of the 1960s before he became an actor. In the 1970s, he began working in stage plays. He also began acting

in movies. At first, he only got small roles. Then, his career took off. Today, Samuel L. Jackson is one of the biggest names in Hollywood. One of his most famous roles was as Mace Windu, in the *Star Wars* movies. Jackson was born in Washington, D.C.

Charles Drew (1904–1950) was an important American scientist. He was born and grew up in Washington, D.C. In the 1930s and 1940s, Drew discovered ways to safely test and store blood, and to organize blood donors. It could then be used in large blood banks. His work helped accident victims and soldiers receive blood, which saved many lives. He also organized and directed medical programs in the United States and Great Britain.

J. Edgar Hoover (1895–1972) directed the Federal Bureau of Investigation (FBI) for almost 50 years. He built a very powerful and effective crime-fighting organization. He helped create and organize the FBI's fingerprint files, and other forensic science laboratories. Toward  the end of his career, Hoover collected information on people who weren't criminals. They were simply people he didn't like. Hoover sometimes collected information illegally. Many people believe he had information about important people like presidents and senators, and that Hoover used that information to expand his power.

The National Mall

One of the most famous parts of Washington, D.C., is the **National Mall and Memorial Parks**. It is a large park where some of the nation's most important buildings and monuments are located. It includes the land between the Lincoln Memorial on the west side and the Capitol building on the east side. The strip of land stretches for almost two miles (3.2 km). Following are some of the most famous buildings in and around the National Mall.

The **Lincoln Memorial** honors Abraham Lincoln, the 16th president of the United States. The memorial includes a large statue of Lincoln sitting in a chair, with a building and information to learn more about him. The memorial was dedicated in 1922. You can see a picture of the Lincoln Memorial on the back of a United States five-dollar bill, and on the back of a penny.

Millions of people visit the Lincoln Memorial each year.

The **Washington Monument** is almost in the center of the National Mall. It is shaped like an Egyptian obelisk, and is 555 feet (169 m) high. It honors George Washington, the first president of the United States. Construction of the monument was finished in 1884. It is the tallest structure in Washington, D.C.

The **World War II Memorial** honors "The Greatest Generation," those Americans who served during World War II (1939–1945). It includes fountains, pavilions, and 56 granite columns. The memorial was dedicated in 2004.

The **Vietnam Veterans Memorial** has two black granite walls, set at an angle, engraved with the names of Americans who died during, or because of injuries from, the Vietnam War (1959–1975). Many people come to find the name of family or friends and make a rubbing of the name.

The **National Archives Building** houses thousands of historic documents. The Declaration of Independence, the Constitution, and the Bill of Rights are on public display in the building's rotunda.

The **Smithsonian Institution** includes several museums. Two of the most popular are the National Museum of Natural History, and the National Air and Space Museum.

The National Museum of Natural History.

The **United States Capitol** building is on the east end of the National Mall. Members of Congress meet in the Capitol to make laws. The north wing of the Capitol houses the U.S. Senate. The south wing houses the U.S. House of Representatives. In the middle of the Capitol is a rotunda, a large circular room covered by a dome. The Capitol is also filled with many paintings, sculptures, and other historic artwork.

The White House

The **White House** is located at 1600 Pennsylvania Avenue, just north of the National Mall. It is where the president of the United States lives and works. In 1792, President George Washington chose the building's architect, James Hoban. Workers began construction, using sandstone from Virginia quarries.

In 1800, President John Adams moved into the White House. He only lived there a short time. Thomas Jefferson, the third president of the United States, was the first president to live there from the beginning of his term. Every president since then has lived and worked in the White House.

Over the years, the White House has had several names, including the President's House, and the Executive Mansion. In 1901, President Theodore Roosevelt gave the White House its current official name.

The White House has six stories, four above ground and two underground. It has 55,000 square feet (5,110 sq m) of floor space.

Top: President Obama meets with Vice President Joe Biden and Ambassador Christopher Hill in the Oval Office. Bottom: President Obama at his desk.

There are 132 rooms, 35 bathrooms, and 3 elevators. It has five full-time chefs, a tennis court, a swimming pool, and a bowling lane. Many foreign officials and ambassadors come to the White House to talk to the president. The public can also tour the White House.

Transportation

Traffic is often crowded in Washington, D.C. There are too many cars for the roads. Huge numbers of people bike, walk, or use public transportation to get to work.

Washington, D.C., has good public transportation. The Metrorail is a train and subway system

The Washington Metrorail subway system is one of the largest rail transit systems in the country.

that serves the city and the surrounding area. People call it "The Metro." There is also a bus system that serves almost 500,000 people daily.

Ronald Reagan Washington National Airport is actually in Virginia, but it is the closest airport to the downtown area. More than 18 million people fly in and out of the airport every year. Other airports that serve the city include Washington Dulles International Airport, in Virginia, and Baltimore-Washington International Thurgood Marshall Airport, which is located in Maryland.

A plane passes the Washington Monument preparing to land at Ronald Reagan Washington National Airport in Arlington, Virginia.

Industry

The main employer in Washington, D.C., is the federal government. About one-third of the city's workers are involved in some part of the

President Obama address a joint session of Congress. Many people in Washington, D.C., are employed by members of Congress.

government. Many people are needed to keep the government running. The president and members of Congress employ many people. Government agencies employ many others. Foreign countries also employ workers. There are more than 160 embassies where ambassadors from other countries work.

Visitors on foot and on Segways, personal two-wheeled motorized people-movers, view the White House. This is one of many sites visited by millions of tourists to the Washington, D.C., area.

The second-most important part of the city's economy is tourism. More than 16 million people visit Washington, D.C., each year. Many visit the city's national monuments and historic sites. Others come to attend conventions held in the city.

There is a small amount of manufacturing in Washington, D.C. The printing and food products industries are the busiest.

Sports

The Washington Redskins play in the National Football League. They have played in five Super Bowls, winning three times. The Washington Nationals play in Major League Baseball. The Washington Wizards play in the National Basketball Association. The team won the NBA Championship in 1978. The Washington Mystics play in the Women's National Basketball Association. The Washington Capitals play in the National Hockey League. The city also hosts a professional soccer team called D.C. United. The team has won the U.S. Open Cup twice.

Washington, D.C., is home to teams of many other sports, including rugby, lacrosse, and fast-pitch softball. Professional tennis events and national marathons are held in Washington, D.C.

The city of Washington has many parks. There is a lot of space available for softball, volleyball, running, and other outdoor activities.

A jogger runs along the National Mall near the Capitol building.

Entertainment

Washington, D.C., is full of museums, theaters, and interesting places to visit. In 1846, Congress created the Smithsonian Institution to maintain the nation's official museums and galleries. The National Museum of Natural History showcases the history of planet Earth, especially the study of life and the study of geology. The National Air and Space Museum highlights the history of airplane flight and space travel.

National Air
and Space Museum

The National Museum of the American Indian displays the history of Native American tribes.

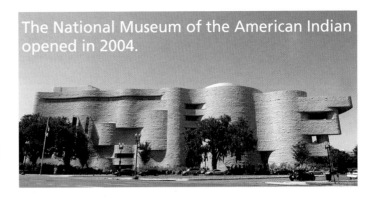
The National Museum of the American Indian opened in 2004.

The National Portrait Gallery includes paintings of many famous Americans, including presidents such as George Washington.

The National Gallery of Art is not part of the Smithsonian. It is totally owned by the U.S. government. It has one of the finest collections of art in the world.

Washington, D.C., is also home to many world-class performing arts institutions. These include the National Symphony Orchestra, the Washington Ballet, the Washington National Opera, and the John F. Kennedy Center for the Performing Arts.

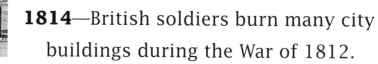

Timeline

Pre-1700s—Piscataway and Powhatan Native Americans live in the Washington, D.C., area.

1790—Congress passes a law to create a site for the new permanent capital.

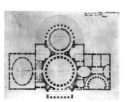

1793—Construction of the Capitol building begins.

1800—The federal government moves to Washington, D.C.

1814—British soldiers burn many city buildings during the War of 1812.

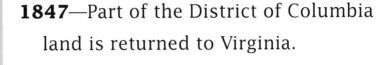

1847—Part of the District of Columbia land is returned to Virginia.

1861–1865—The Civil War. Union troops protect the city from Confederate forces.

1884—Construction of the Washington Monument is completed.

1922—The Lincoln Memorial is dedicated.

1943—The Jefferson Memorial is dedicated.

2001—A terrorist attack destroys part of the Pentagon building.

Glossary

Ambassador—A person who represents another country.

Architect—A person who creates the plans to make something, such as a building or a city.

Civil War—The war fought between America's Northern and Southern states from 1861-1865. The Southern states were for slavery. They wanted to start their own country. Northern states fought against slavery and a division of the country.

District of Columbia—A piece of land set aside to house the federal government.

Forensic Science—A science that examines clues at crime scenes with the objective of proving who performed a crime. Methods include lifting fingerprints and footprints, collecting hair and fibers, and examining biological evidence, such as drops of blood.

Infest—To be full of large numbers of bugs or other pests, which often cause damage to other nearby living things.

Obelisk—A tall, narrow, four-sided monument with a pyramid shape on top.

Pierre L'Enfant—The architect who initially designed the city of Washington, D.C.

Reservoir—A lake, either man-made or natural, that is often used as a source of water for a nearby city.

Rubbing—Taking an impression of something by placing a piece of paper on top of the design, then using a crayon or pencil to rub over the paper. People often take rubbings of names on the Vietnam Veterans Memorial.

Smithsonian Institution—An organization created by Congress in 1846 to maintain the nation's official museums and galleries. There are several Smithsonian-run museums located in Washington, D.C. They are very popular tourist destinations.

Index

A
Adams, John 34
Alexandria 10, 18
America 4
Anacostia River 8
Arlington County 23

B
Baltimore-Washington
    International
    Thurgood Marshall
    Airport 37
Bill of Rights 32

C
Capitol (building) 10,
    20, 28, 33
Civil War 20
Columbus, Christopher
    4
Confederates 20
Congress, U.S. 19, 22,
    33, 38, 42
Constitution, U.S. 32

D
Dalecarlia Reservoir 8
D.C. United 40
Declaration of
    Independence 32
Department of
    Defense, U.S. 23
District of Columbia 4,
    8, 10, 20
Drew, Charles 26

E
Earth 42
Ellington, Duke 24
England 19
Executive Mansion 35

F
Federal Bureau of
    Investigation (FBI)
    27
Federal City 10
Foggy Bottom 18
Franklin Delano
    Roosevelt Memorial
    16

G
Georgetown 10, 18, 20
Georgetown Reservoir
    8
Great Britain 26

H
Hamburgh 10, 18
Hoban, James 34
Hollywood, CA 25
Hoover, J. Edgar 27
House of
    Representatives,
    U.S. 33

J
Jackson, Samuel L. 25
Japan 14, 15
Jefferson, Thomas 34
Jefferson Memorial 16
John F. Kennedy Center
    for the Performing
    Arts 43

K
Korean War Veterans
    Memorial 16

L
L'Enfant, Pierre 10
Library of Congress 21
Lincoln, Abraham 29
Lincoln Memorial 21,
    28, 29

M
Major League Baseball
    40
Maryland 8, 18, 19, 37
McMillan Reservoir 8
Metrorail 36

N
National Air and Space
    Museum 32, 42
National Archives
    Building 32
National Basketball
    Association 40
National Cherry
    Blossom Festival
    14, 17
National Football
    League 40
National Gallery of
    Art 43
National Hockey
    League 40
National Mall and
    Memorial Parks 28,
    30, 33, 34
National Museum of
    Natural History 32,
    42
National Museum of
    the American Indian
    43
National Portrait
    Gallery 43
National Symphony
    Orchestra 43
NBA Championship 40
New York City, NY 23

P
Pentagon 23
Piscataway (tribe) 18
Point Reno 10
Potomac River 8, 10,
    18, 19, 20, 23
Powhatan (tribe) 18
President's House 35

R
Ronald Reagan
    Washington National
    Airport 37
Roosevelt, Theodore
    35

S
Scidmore, Eliza
    Ruhamah 14
Senate, U.S. 33

Smithsonian Institution
    32, 42, 43
Star Wars 25
Super Bowl 40

T
Taft, William Howard 16
Tenleytown 10

U
United States 4, 10, 15,
    16, 19, 23, 24, 26, 29,
    30, 33, 34, 43
U.S. Open Cup 40

V
Vietnam Veterans
    Memorial 31
Vietnam War 31
Virginia 8, 18, 19, 20, 23,
    34, 37

W
War of 1812 20
Washington, George 10,
    19, 30, 34, 43
Washington Ballet 43
Washington Capitals 40
Washington Dulles
    International Airport
    37
Washington Monument
    21, 30
Washington Mystics 40
Washington National
    Opera 43
Washington Nationals 40
Washington Redskins 40
Washington Wizards 40
West Potomac Park 16
White House 20, 34, 35
Windu, Mace 25
Women's National
    Basketball Association
    40
World Trade Center 23
World War I 21
World War II 21, 31
World War II Memorial 31